Early Morning in the Street

The sky was bright
And wide awake,
The street was bright
And sunny.
And I was bright
And wide awake,
All hoppity
And runny.
I wonder if
The sky and street
Thought that I
Was funny.

Kay Dee

Little People™ Big Book

About WHERE WE LIVE

TIME LIFE for Children™

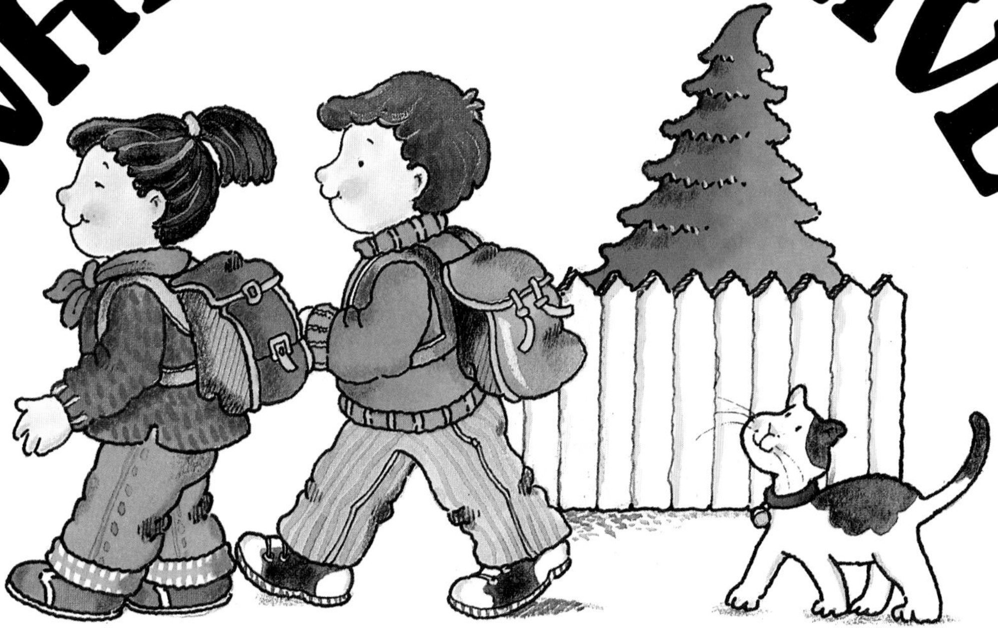

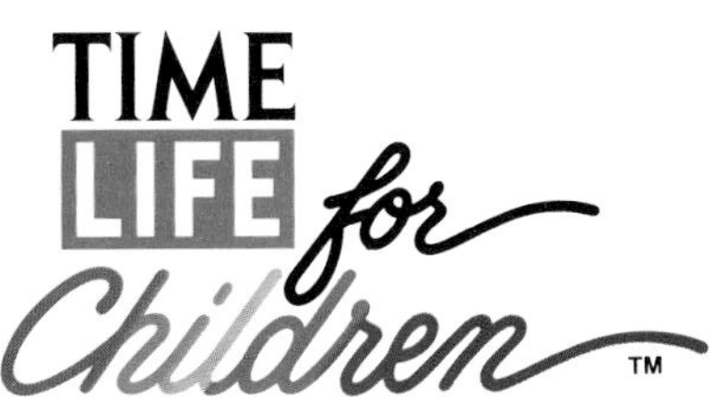

ALEXANDRIA, VIRGINIA

Table of Contents

Around the Corner and Down the Street

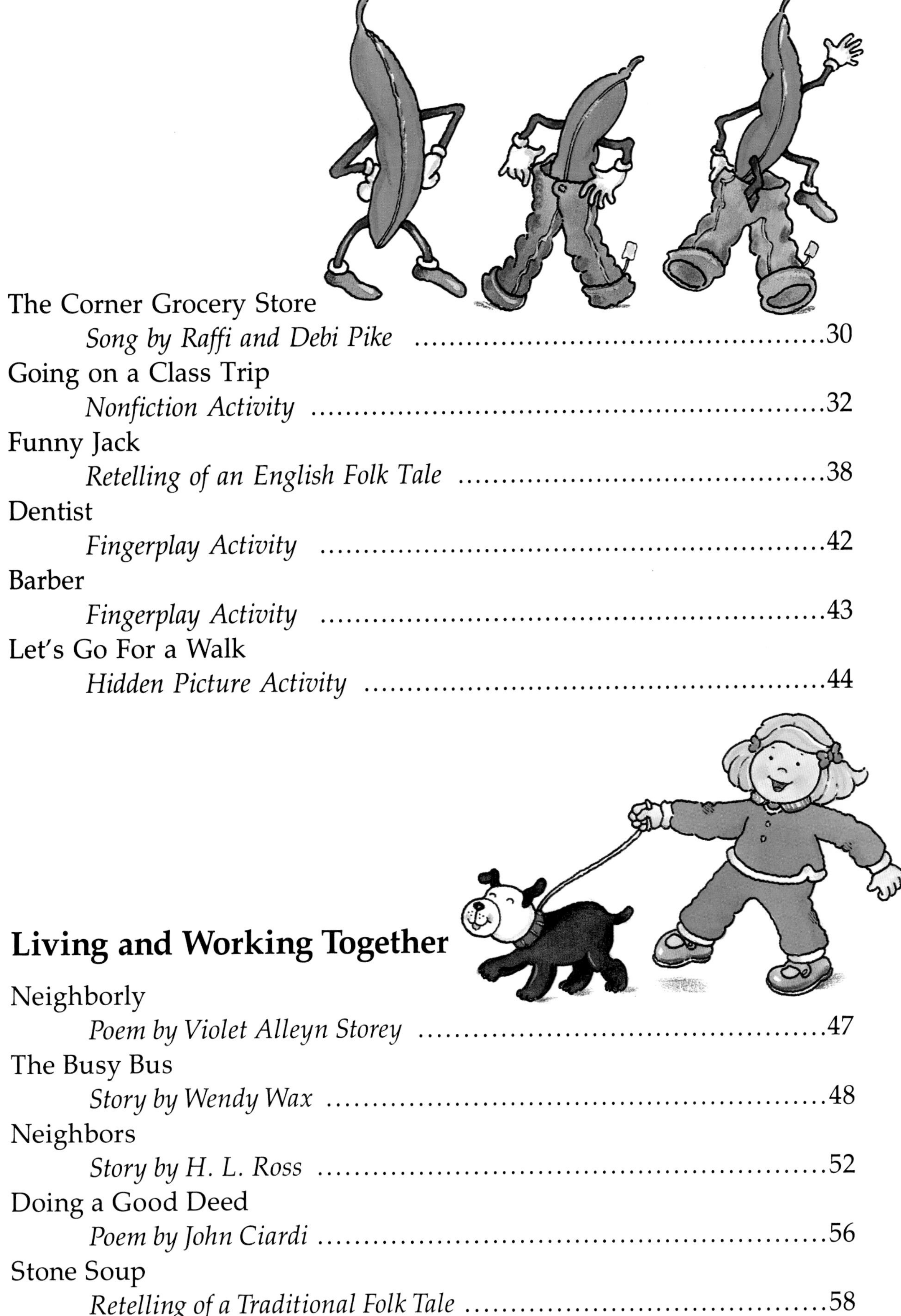

Living and Working Together

My House and Your House

Our House

Our house is small—
The lawn and all
Can scarcely hold the flowers,
Yet every bit,
The whole of it,
Is precious, for it's ours!

From door to door,
From roof to floor,
From wall to wall we love it;
We wouldn't change
For something strange
One shabby corner of it!

The space complete
In cubic feet
From cellar floor to rafter
Just measures right,
And not too tight,
For us, and friends, and laughter!

Dorothy Brown Thompson

Where Do You Live?

Out in the country lives Darin McDabbin,
So comfy and cozy in his little log cabin.

And just down the road lives old Farmer Ben,
His nearest of neighbors are pigs in a pen.

Of course, city folks like Bea and Bob Brown
Live in high-rise apartments all over the town.

The Browns' next-door neighbor is Mary Malone.
She lives with her mom in a house made of stone.

The traveling Tuttles would much rather roam—
To live here and there in a long mobile home.

And the Carroway family is always afloat,
Cruising the river in a shipshape houseboat.

But no one's as happy as Hildegard Kraus,
Whose favorite place is her plain, homey house!

Where do you live—on land or on sea?
And whose weekend guest would you most like to be?

Teddy Slater

The City Mouse and the Country Mouse

A Retelling of a Fable by Aesop

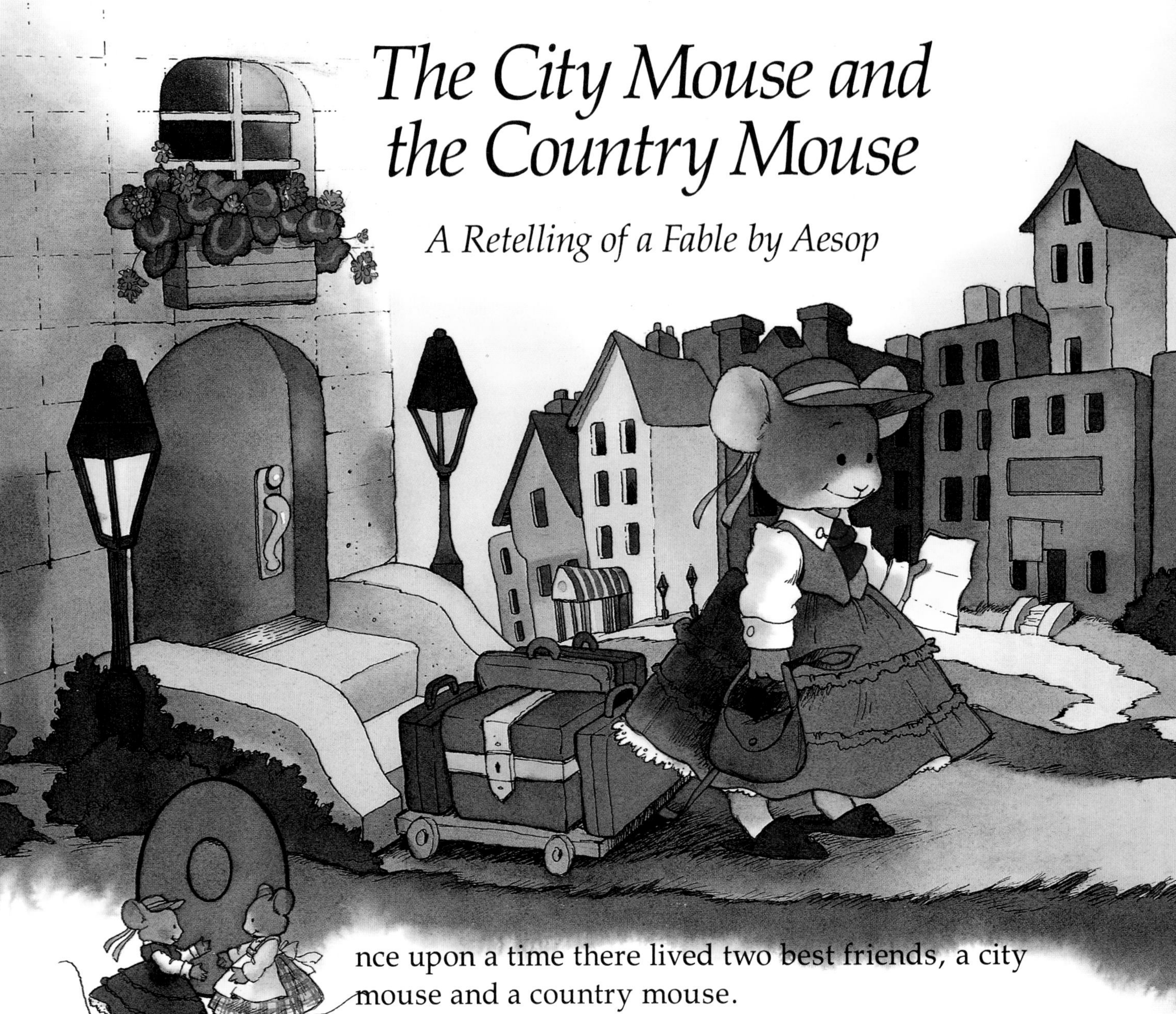

Once upon a time there lived two best friends, a city mouse and a country mouse.

The city mouse lived in a beautiful mansion on a tree-lined street in the most elegant section of a busy town. Most days she'd spend cuddling up in an easy chair, warming herself in front of the cozy living-room fireplace. As the firelight flickered off the polished wooden floor, she'd dream of nibbling bonbons at elegant luncheons.

One day, the city mouse received a letter from her best friend, inviting her to come to the country for a visit. The city mouse was very excited. That day, she had no time to lounge about in front of the fire—she was much too busy. Instead, she spent all day packing. "I hope I have packed enough clothes," she thought to herself, struggling to zip up a suitcase.

While the city mouse spent her day preparing for her journey, the country mouse spent her day cleaning her simple house that stood beneath a shady oak tree. Beautiful wild flowers grew in her front yard, and a lovely stream flowed nearby.

The next day the city mouse arrived in the country pulling a cart with four suitcases and a trunk.

"Welcome, my dear friend," said the country mouse, giving her friend a hug. "I'm so happy to see you. Let me show you around the country."

So the two mice set off for a walk. Soon they came upon some acorns. "Help me fill this basket with acorns," said the country mouse. "They are delicious. We can have some for dinner."

"Yuck," thought the city mouse to herself, pulling along the basket filled with acorns.

Then they came to the vegetable patch.

"Oh, wonderful," said the country mouse. "Help me pick some fresh cabbage leaves."

"Do you always work so hard for your dinner?" asked the city mouse, holding her nose at the smell of the cabbage.

At last they came to the quiet stream.

"Come on, let's jump in and cool our feet," shouted the country mouse.

"Oh, no," cried the city mouse. "I'll get my clothes wet."

"Well, let's just sit down for a while and watch the bees and flowers, then," the country mouse said.

"Sit in the dirt? Never!" answered the city mouse. "Anyway, it sounds awfully dull. Let's go home and have dinner. I'm tired and hungry from all this walking."

Back home, the city mouse relaxed while the country mouse prepared dinner. Then she spread a tablecloth on the floor and put out her best plates. As soon as everything was ready, the two friends sat down to a dinner of potato and cabbage soup, freshly baked corn bread, Swiss cheese, and walnuts. For dessert they had fresh blueberries.

While the country mouse hungrily gobbled down her dinner, the city mouse ate very little. Oh, she picked a little here and ate a little there, but the food was much too simple for her taste. After a while the city mouse said, "My dear friend, please don't be offended, but how do you stand it here? It's so quiet—so dull. If we were in the city, I'd serve you the feast of your life. Wait, I have an idea! Why don't you come back to the city with me?"

And the next day, the two mice set off for the city. The country mouse carried a small knapsack and the city mouse pulled along the cart with four suitcases and a trunk. When they reached the city, the country mouse was amazed at the sight of the tall buildings, the noisy cars, and the many people.

At last they reached a row of elegant houses.

"This is where I live," said the city mouse proudly.

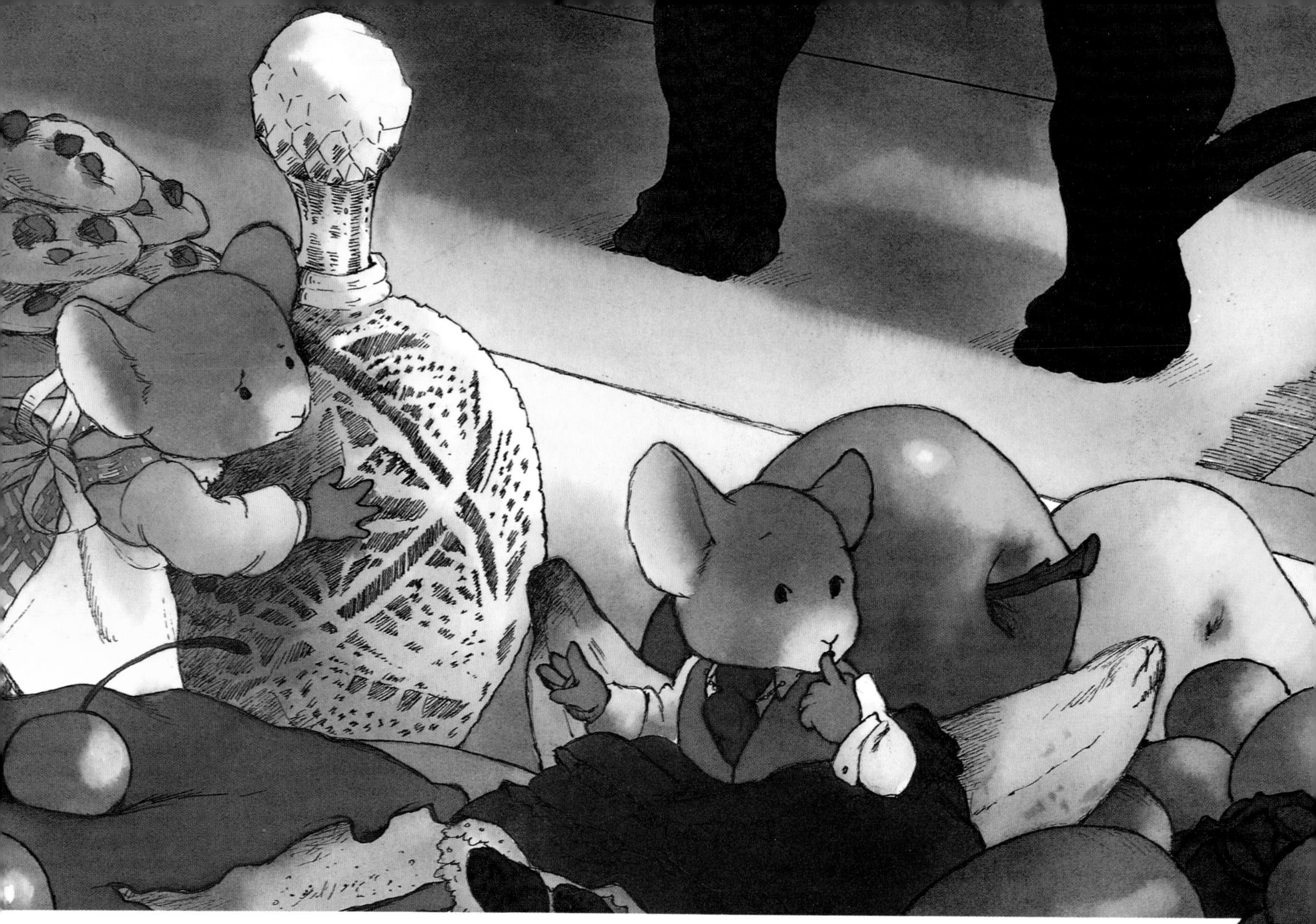

The country mouse was indeed impressed. They went up a flight of marble steps that led to a polished wooden door. Two lamps glowed brightly on either side of the doorway and lit the entrance.

Once inside the country mouse marveled at the huge grandfather clock in the front hallway. Suddenly the clock struck seven o'clock, and both mice jumped with surprise. Holding their ears, the two mice set off for the grand dining room.

"How elegant all this is!" said the country mouse.

At last it was dinnertime. The two mice feasted on figs, honey, cakes, and cookies. They laughed and told stories as they ate from china plates that gleamed in the candlelight.

"This is magnificent!" exclaimed the country mouse, thoroughly enjoying herself.

Suddenly they heard heavy footsteps and the door to the dining room burst open. "Quick!" said the city mouse. "We must hide!"

The two mice scampered into a corner of the table and hid. The country mouse was shaking with fear.

After a while, the city mouse, who had remained quite calm, peeked out to see if the room was safe. "It's okay to come out now,"

she said, helping her quivering friend back to the banquet. But, just then they heard a dog barking.

"Run!" shouted the city mouse. And once again, the two mice scampered across the table to their hiding place. Never had the country mouse been so frightened in her whole life!

When the dog had gone, the country mouse quickly packed up her knapsack.

"My food may be simple and my home may be plain," she explained, "but at least I can eat my dinner in peace. I am going back to the country. Good-bye, my friend."

"My life may be dangerous," said the city mouse, "but I do prefer to live here in the city. Good-bye, dear friend. Please visit me again if your life gets too dull."

"And you must come again to the country when you want some peace."

And so the country mouse set off for the peaceful countryside while the city mouse prepared for sleep in her elegant bed.

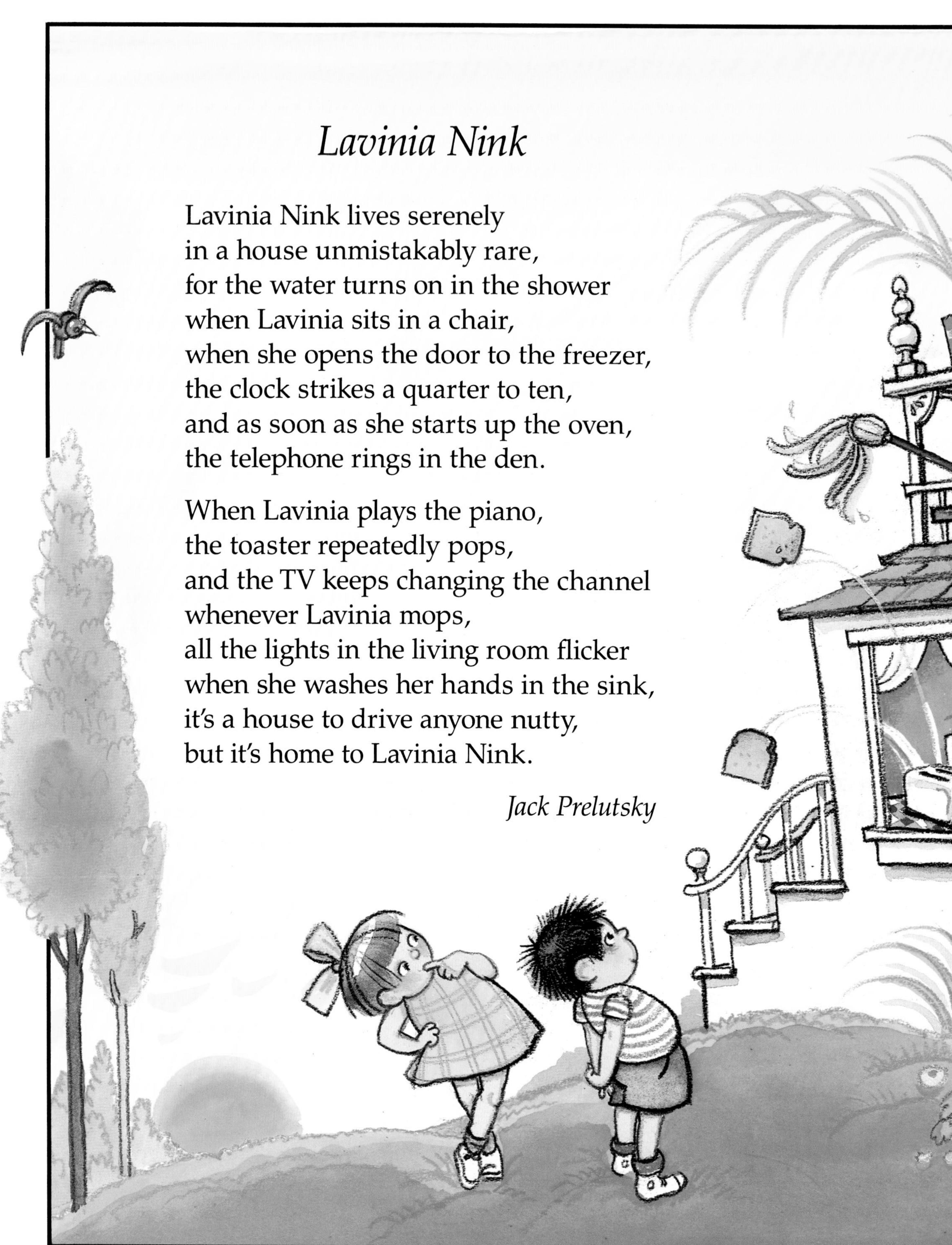

Lavinia Nink

Lavinia Nink lives serenely
in a house unmistakably rare,
for the water turns on in the shower
when Lavinia sits in a chair,
when she opens the door to the freezer,
the clock strikes a quarter to ten,
and as soon as she starts up the oven,
the telephone rings in the den.

When Lavinia plays the piano,
the toaster repeatedly pops,
and the TV keeps changing the channel
whenever Lavinia mops,
all the lights in the living room flicker
when she washes her hands in the sink,
it's a house to drive anyone nutty,
but it's home to Lavinia Nink.

Jack Prelutsky

ZAP.P.P.

The Big Orange Splot

by Daniel Manus Pinkwater

Mr. Plumbean lived on a street where all the houses were the same.

He liked it that way. So did everybody else on Mr. Plumbean's street. "This is a neat street," they would say. Then one day . . .

A seagull flew over Mr. Plumbean's house. He was carrying a can of bright orange paint. (No one knows why.) And he dropped the can (no one knows why) right over Mr. Plumbean's house.

It made a big orange splot on Mr. Plumbean's house.

"Oooooh! Too bad!" everybody said. "Mr. Plumbean will have to paint his house again."

"I suppose I will," said Mr. Plumbean. But he didn't paint his house right away. He looked at the big orange splot for a long time; then he went about his business.

The neighbors got tired of seeing that big orange splot. Someone said, "Mr. Plumbean, we wish you'd get around to painting your house."

"O.K.," said Mr. Plumbean.

He got some blue paint and some white paint, and that night he got busy. He painted at night because it was cooler.

When the paint was gone, the roof was blue. The walls were white. And the big orange splot was still there.

Then he got some more paint. He got red paint, yellow paint, green paint, and purple paint.

In the morning the other people on the street came out of their houses. Their houses were all the same. But Mr. Plumbean's house was like a rainbow. It was like a jungle. It was like an explosion.

There was the big orange splot. And there were little orange splots. There were stripes. There were pictures of elephants and lions and pretty girls and steamshovels.

The people said, "Plumbean has popped his cork, flipped his wig, blown his stack, and dropped his stopper." They went away muttering.

That day Mr. Plumbean bought carpenter's tools. That night he built a tower on top of his roof, and he painted a clock on the tower.

The next day the people said, "Plumbean has gushed his mush, lost his marbles, and slipped his hawser." They decided they would pretend not to notice.

That very night Mr. Plumbean got a truck full of green things. He planted palm trees, baobabs, thorn bushes, onions, and frangipani. In the morning he bought a hammock and an alligator.

When the other people came out of their houses, they saw Mr. Plumbean swinging in a hammock between two palm trees. They saw an alligator lying in the grass. Mr. Plumbean was drinking lemonade.

"Plumbean has gone too far!"

"This used to be a neat street!"

"Plumbean, what have you done to your house?" the people shouted.

"My house is me and I am it. My house is where I like to be, and it looks like all my dreams," Mr. Plumbean said.

The people went away. They asked the man who lived next door to Mr. Plumbean to go and have a talk with him. "Tell him that we all liked it here before he changed his house. Tell him that his house has to be the same as ours so we can have a neat street."

The man went to see Mr. Plumbean that evening. They sat under the palm trees drinking lemonade and talking all night long.

Early the next morning the man went out to get lumber and rope and nails and paint. When the people came out of their houses they saw a red and yellow ship next door to the house of Mr. Plumbean.

"What have you done to your house?" they shouted at the man.

"My house is me and I am it. My house is where I like to be, and it looks like all my dreams," said the man, who had always loved ships.

"He's just like Plumbean!" the people said. "He's got bees in his bonnet, bats in his belfry, and knots in his noodle!"

Then, one by one, they went to see Mr. Plumbean, late at night. They would sit under the palm trees and drink lemonade and talk about their dreams—and whenever anybody visited Mr. Plumbean's house, the very next day that person would set about changing his own house to fit his dreams.

Whenever a stranger came to the street of Mr. Plumbean and his neighbors, the stranger would say, "This is not a neat street."

Then all the people would say, "Our street is us and we are it. Our street is where we like to be, and it looks like all our dreams."

STREET GAMES

What's the best thing about a neighborhood? Getting together with all the children to play games like these!

Hopscotch

These children made their hopscotch box with chalk. You can make one, too.

Here's how to play:

Toss a rock into box 1. (Always be careful when you toss the rock. You don't want to hurt anyone.) Then, hop on one foot over box 1, into box 2. When there's one box, land on one foot; when there are two boxes, land on two feet. Hop all the way to REST, and turn around. Then hop back. When you reach box 2, lean over and pick up your rock. Then, hop over box 1, landing on both feet at HOME.

If you make no mistakes, go again—this time tossing your rock into box 2. If you make a mistake, it's the next child's turn. Whoever gets his rock to REST first, wins.

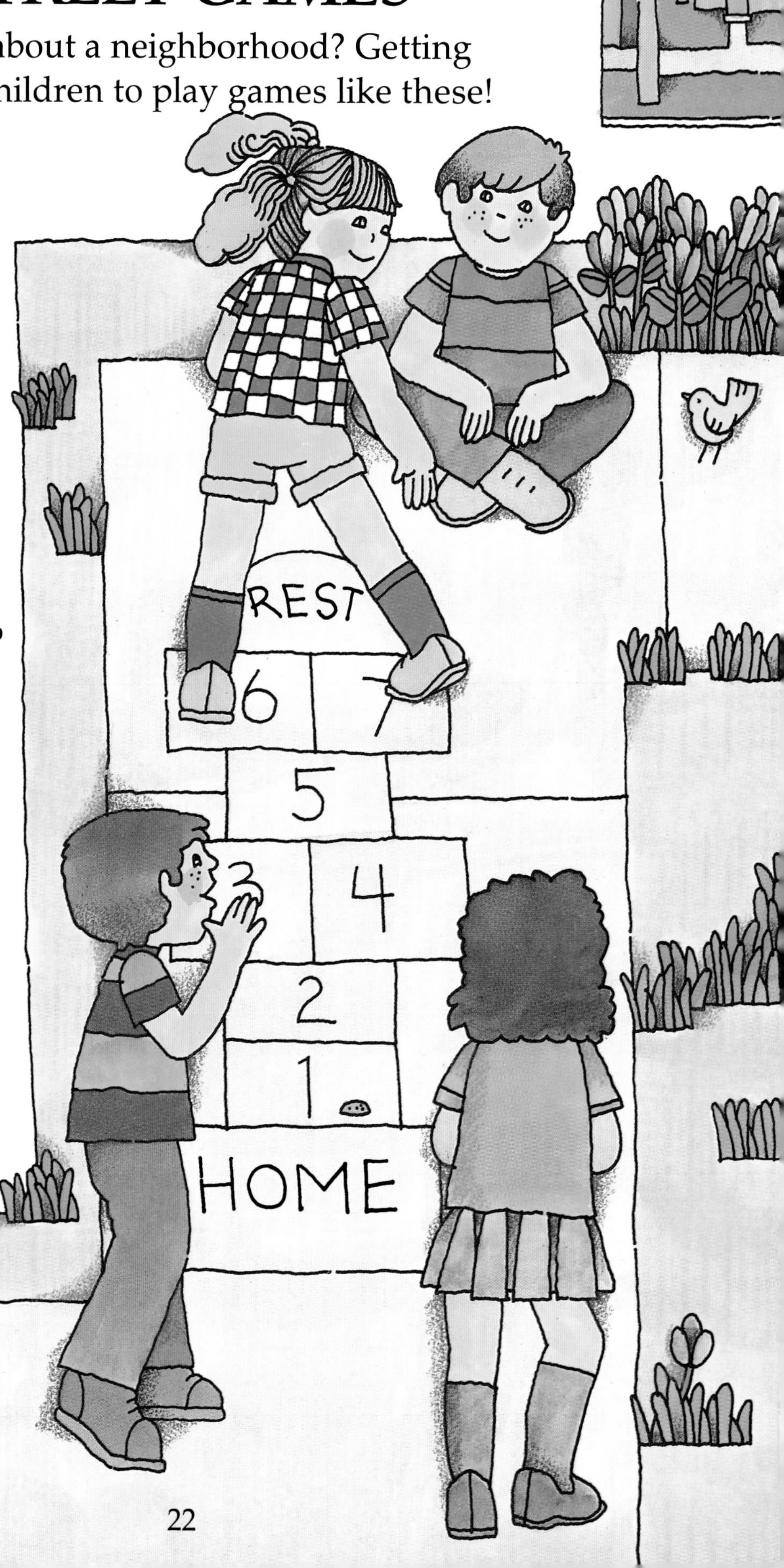

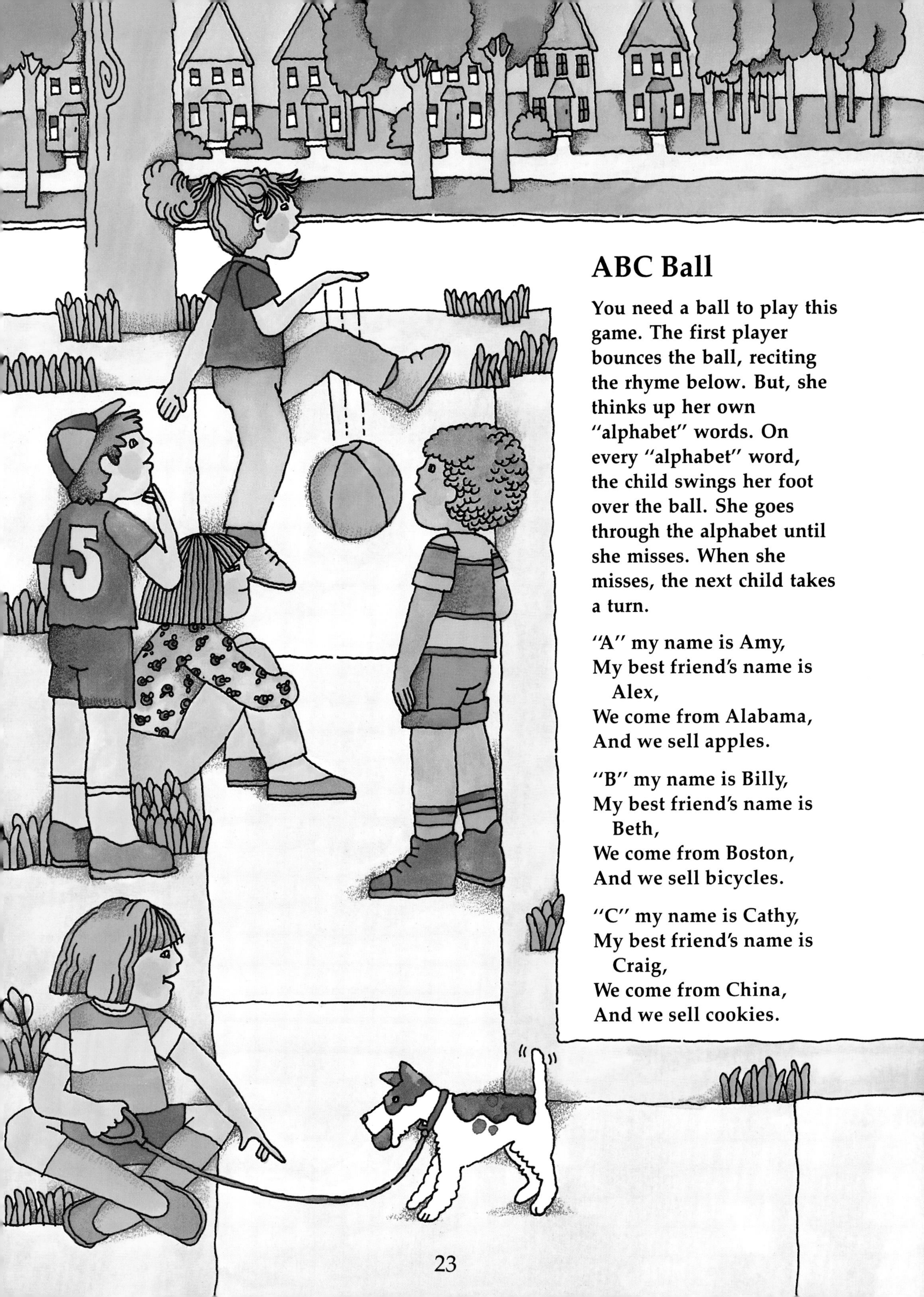

ABC Ball

You need a ball to play this game. The first player bounces the ball, reciting the rhyme below. But, she thinks up her own "alphabet" words. On every "alphabet" word, the child swings her foot over the ball. She goes through the alphabet until she misses. When she misses, the next child takes a turn.

"A" my name is Amy,
My best friend's name is
Alex,
We come from Alabama,
And we sell apples.

"B" my name is Billy,
My best friend's name is
Beth,
We come from Boston,
And we sell bicycles.

"C" my name is Cathy,
My best friend's name is
Craig,
We come from China,
And we sell cookies.

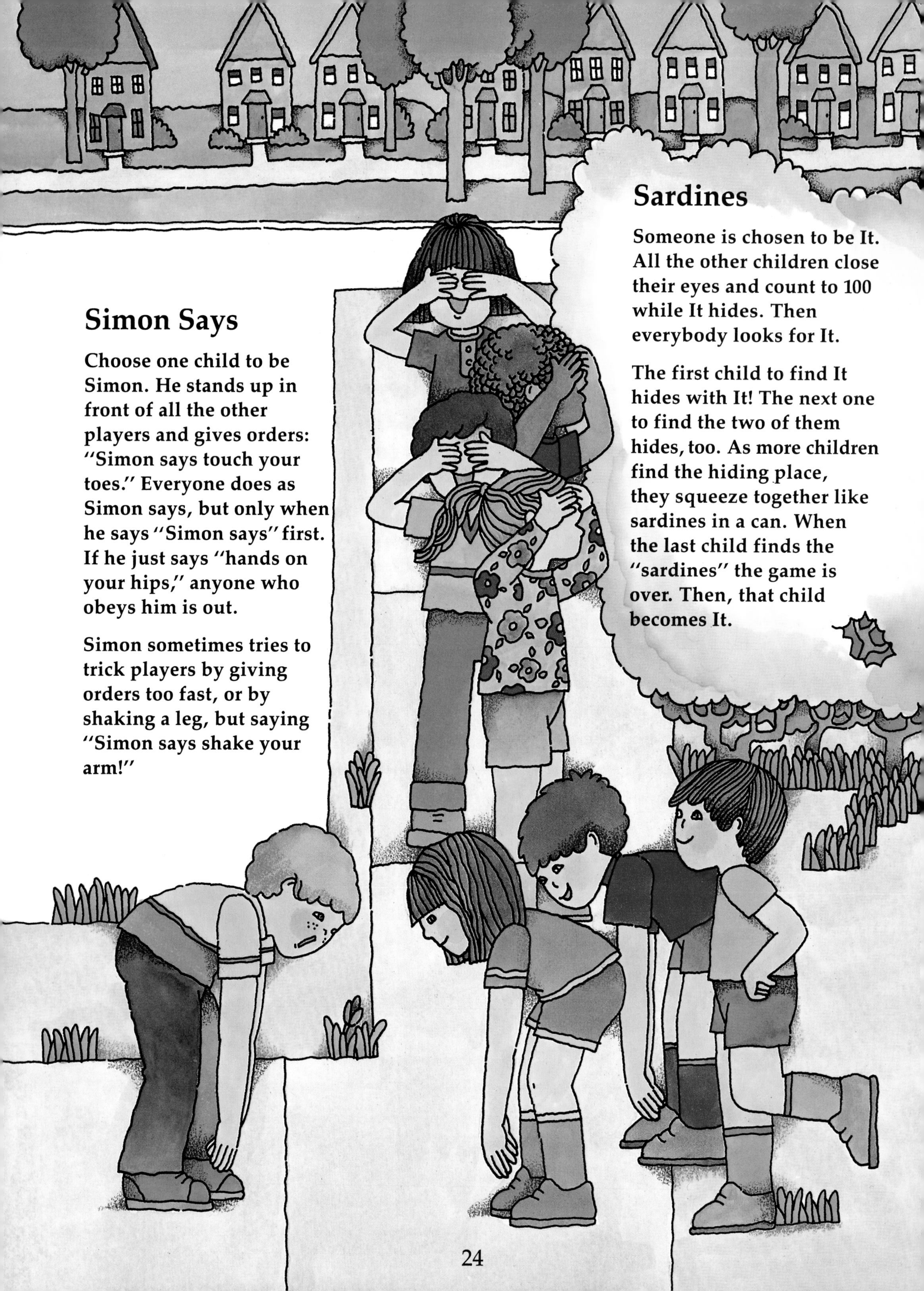

Simon Says

Choose one child to be Simon. He stands up in front of all the other players and gives orders: "Simon says touch your toes." Everyone does as Simon says, but only when he says "Simon says" first. If he just says "hands on your hips," anyone who obeys him is out.

Simon sometimes tries to trick players by giving orders too fast, or by shaking a leg, but saying "Simon says shake your arm!"

Sardines

Someone is chosen to be It. All the other children close their eyes and count to 100 while It hides. Then everybody looks for It.

The first child to find It hides with It! The next one to find the two of them hides, too. As more children find the hiding place, they squeeze together like sardines in a can. When the last child finds the "sardines" the game is over. Then, that child becomes It.

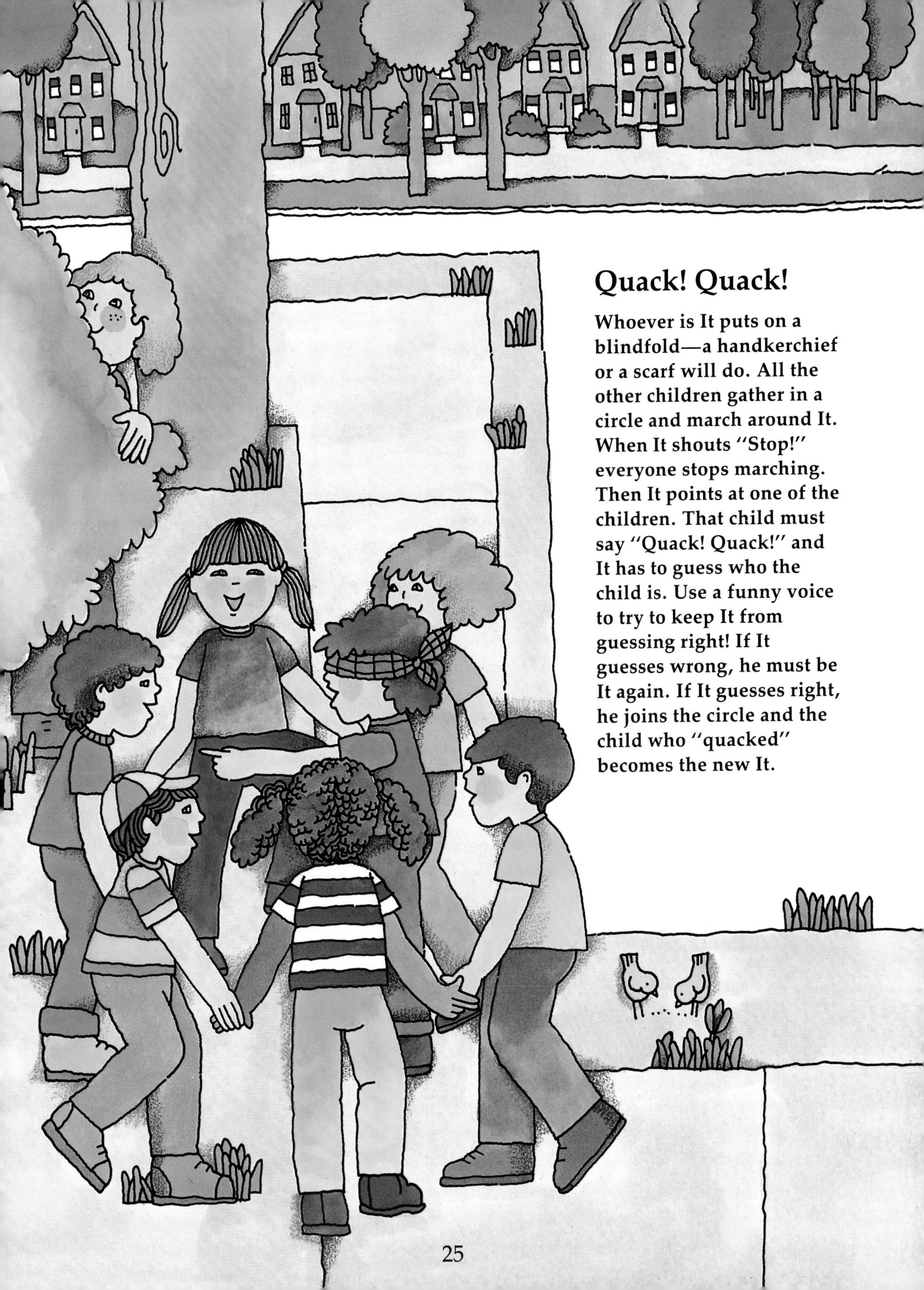

Quack! Quack!

Whoever is It puts on a blindfold—a handkerchief or a scarf will do. All the other children gather in a circle and march around It. When It shouts "Stop!" everyone stops marching. Then It points at one of the children. That child must say "Quack! Quack!" and It has to guess who the child is. Use a funny voice to try to keep It from guessing right! If It guesses wrong, he must be It again. If It guesses right, he joins the circle and the child who "quacked" becomes the new It.

Around the Corner and Down the Street

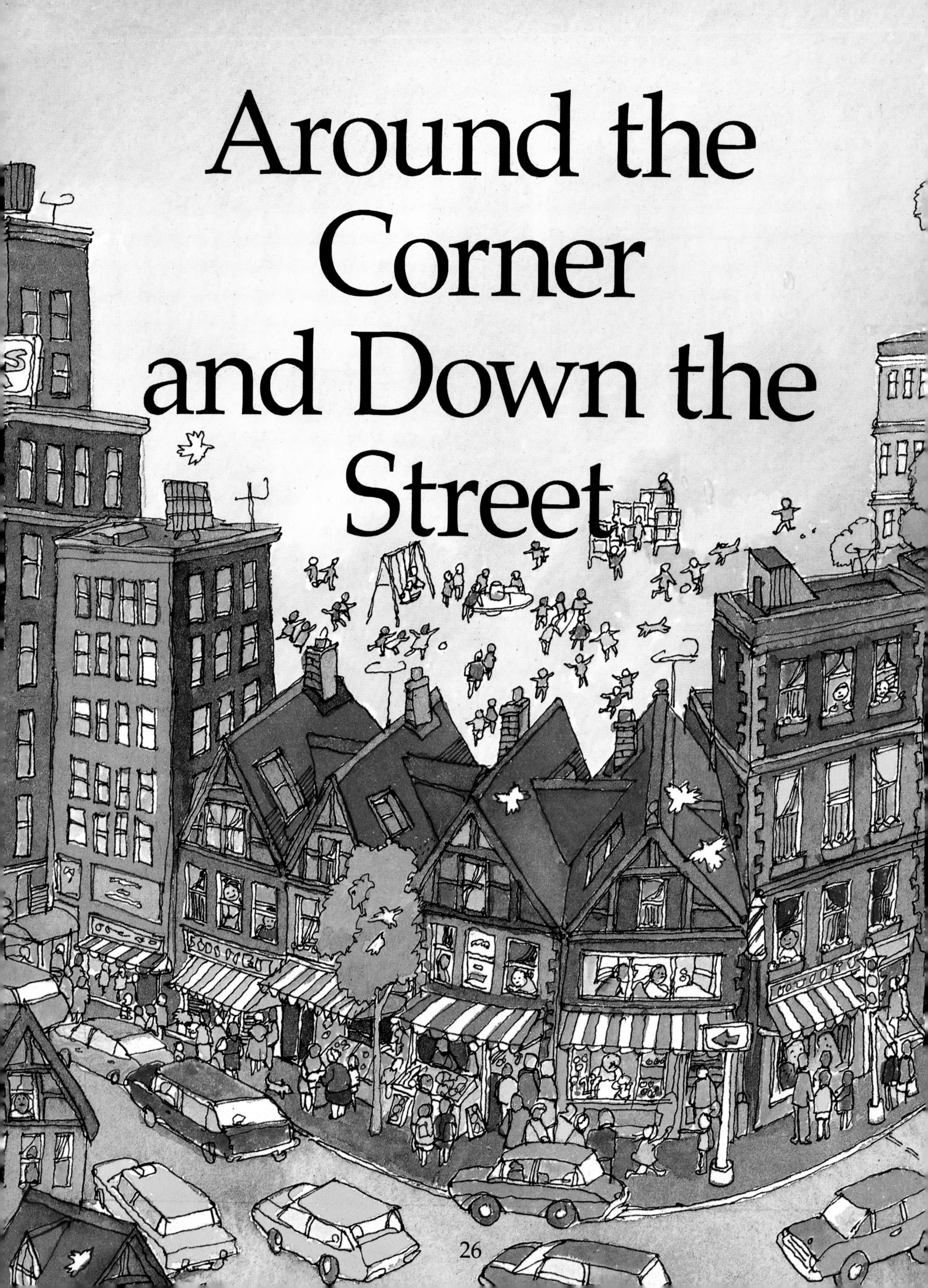

In My Neighborhood

In my neighborhood
It's nice.
We meet
At the candy store
And laugh and buy
One Pepsi for three.
It's O.K. with Mr. Santos.
In my neighborhood
There's a playground
With swings,
And a new climbing thing
Like a tree house.
It's great to climb up high
In my neighborhood
There are people I know
On the block.
I know a lady
Who sells the cloth
My mother buys:
Red and yellow,
Shining flowered cloth.
I know the pickle man.
Sometimes—
He gives me a pickle!
In my neighborhood
It's very nice.

Virginia Schonborg

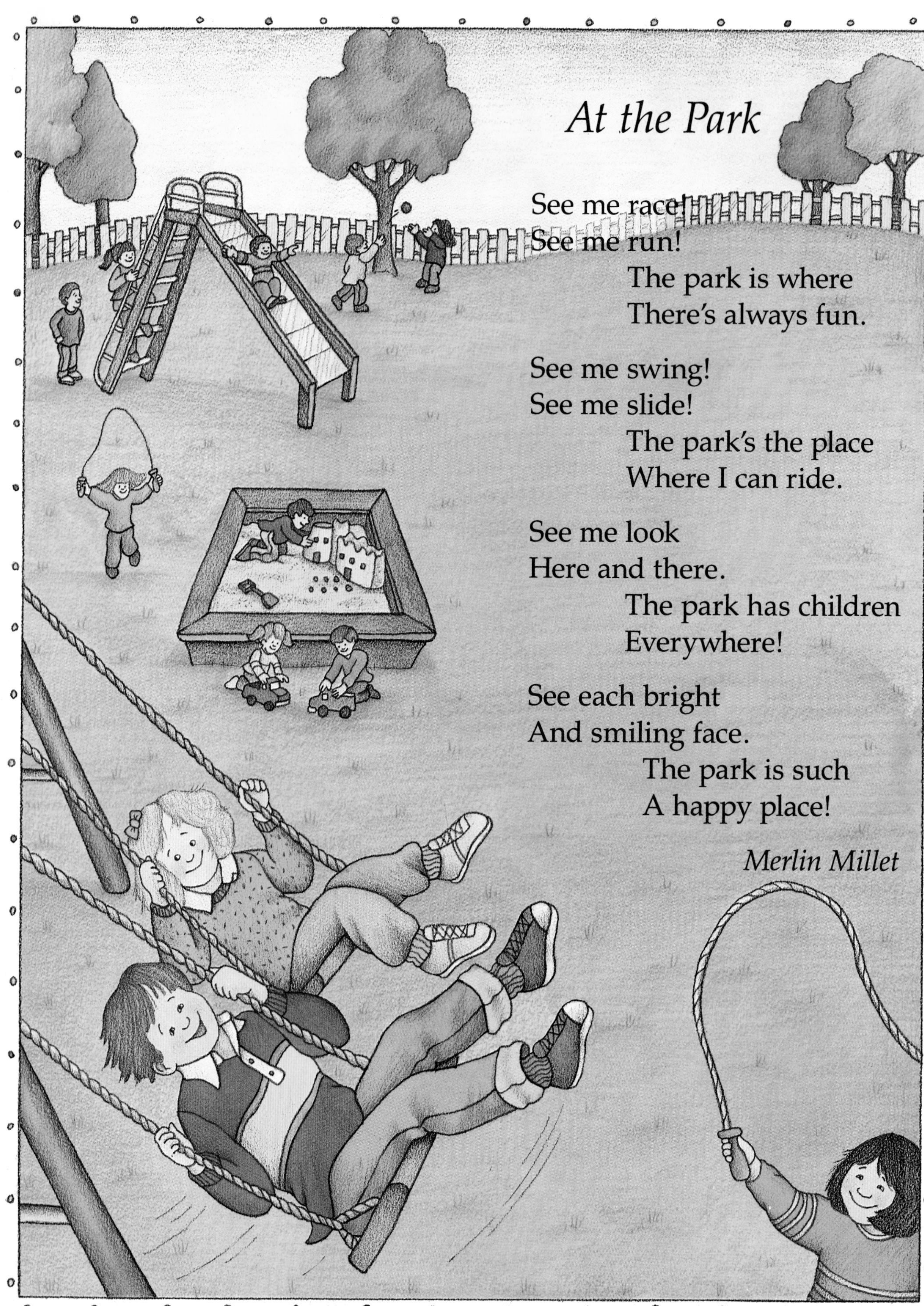

At the Park

See me race!
See me run!
    The park is where
    There's always fun.

See me swing!
See me slide!
    The park's the place
    Where I can ride.

See me look
Here and there.
    The park has children
    Everywhere!

See each bright
And smiling face.
    The park is such
    A happy place!

Merlin Millet

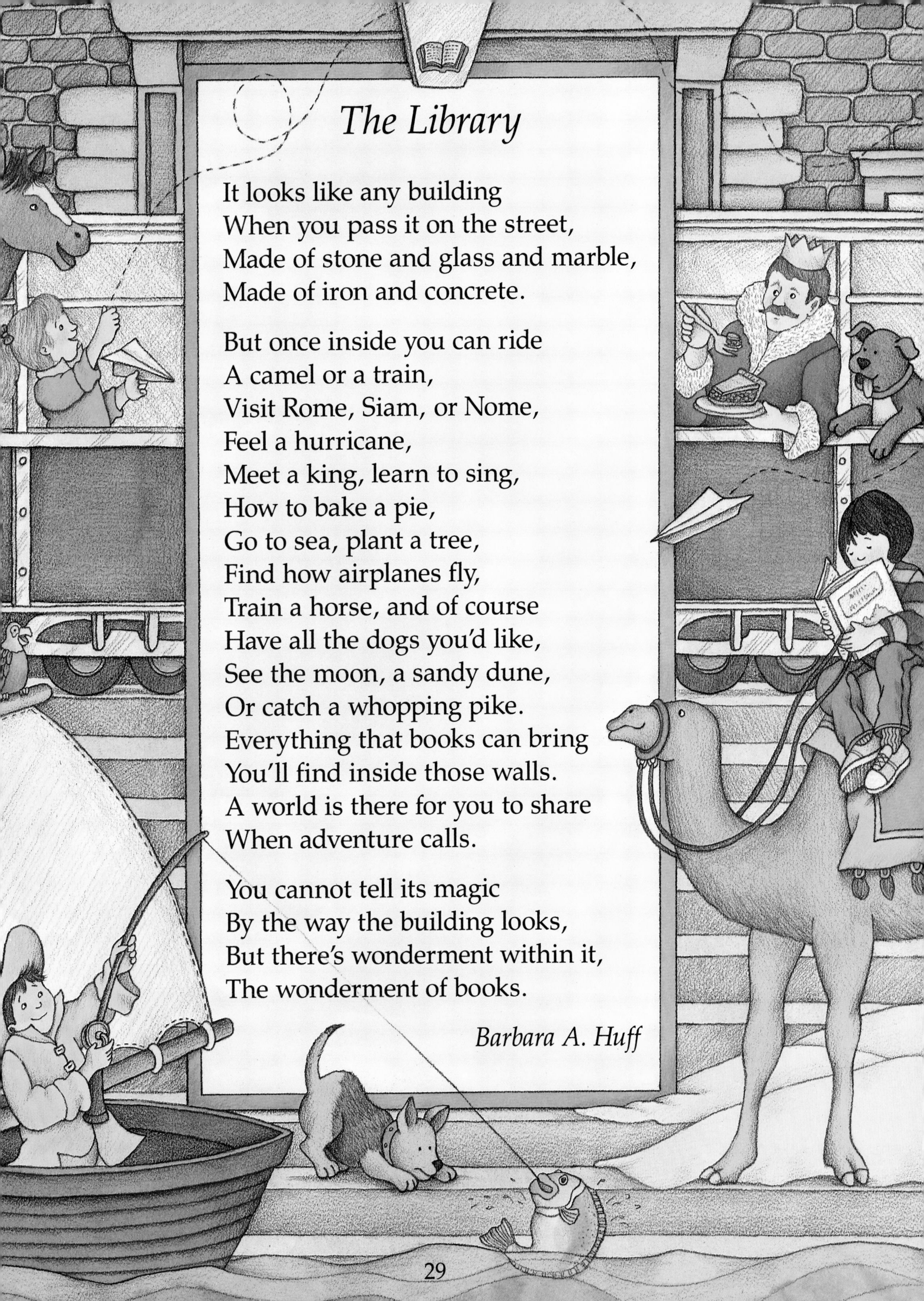

The Library

It looks like any building
When you pass it on the street,
Made of stone and glass and marble,
Made of iron and concrete.

But once inside you can ride
A camel or a train,
Visit Rome, Siam, or Nome,
Feel a hurricane,
Meet a king, learn to sing,
How to bake a pie,
Go to sea, plant a tree,
Find how airplanes fly,
Train a horse, and of course
Have all the dogs you'd like,
See the moon, a sandy dune,
Or catch a whopping pike.
Everything that books can bring
You'll find inside those walls.
A world is there for you to share
When adventure calls.

You cannot tell its magic
By the way the building looks,
But there's wonderment within it,
The wonderment of books.

Barbara A. Huff

The Corner Grocery Store

There was cheese, cheese,
walkin' on its knees,
In the store,
in the store.
There was cheese, cheese,
walkin' on its knees,
In the corner grocery store.

My eyes are dim,
I cannot see,
I have not brought
my specs with me,
I have not brought
my specs with me.

There were plums, plums,
twiddling their thumbs,
In the store,
in the store.
There were plums, plums,
twiddling their thumbs,
In the corner grocery store.

My eyes are dim,
I cannot see,
I have not brought
my specs with me,
I have not brought
my specs with me.

There was corn, corn,
blowin' on a horn,
In the store,
in the store.
There was corn, corn,
blowin' on a horn,
In the corner grocery store.

My eyes are dim,
I cannot see,
I have not brought
my specs with me,
I have not brought
my specs with me.

There were beans, beans,
tryin' on some jeans,
In the store,
in the store.
There were beans, beans,
tryin' on some jeans,
In the corner grocery store.

My eyes are dim,
I cannot see,
I have not brought
my specs with me,
I have not brought
my specs with me.

There was more, more,
just inside the door,
In the store,
in the store.
There was more, more,
just inside the door,
In the corner grocery store.

My eyes are dim,
I cannot see,
I have not brought
my specs with me,
I have not brought
my specs with me.

Raffi and Debi Pike

GOING ON A CLASS TRIP

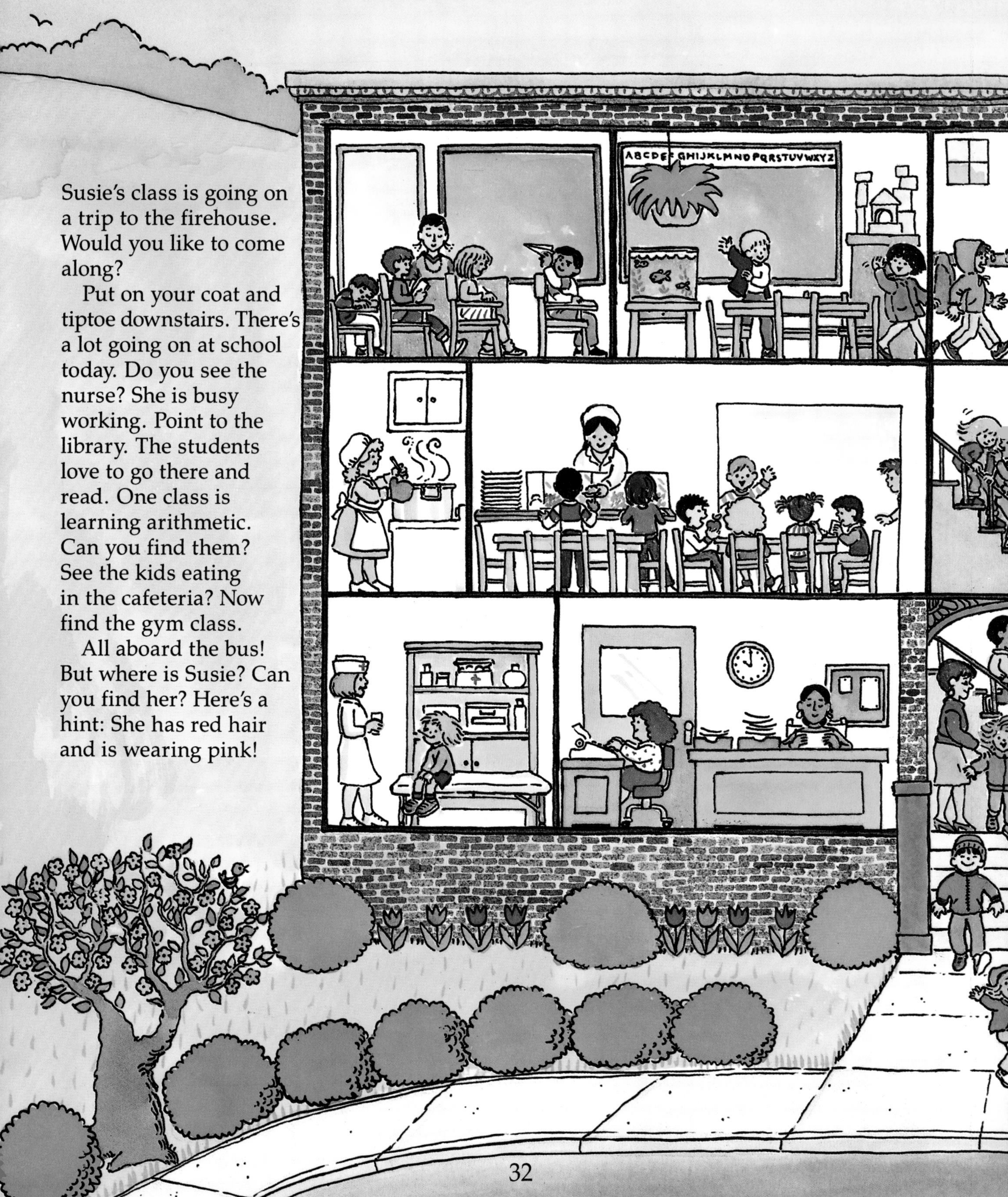

Susie's class is going on a trip to the firehouse. Would you like to come along?

Put on your coat and tiptoe downstairs. There's a lot going on at school today. Do you see the nurse? She is busy working. Point to the library. The students love to go there and read. One class is learning arithmetic. Can you find them? See the kids eating in the cafeteria? Now find the gym class.

All aboard the bus! But where is Susie? Can you find her? Here's a hint: She has red hair and is wearing pink!

2
+1

Here we are at the firehouse! It's fun to climb on the bright red truck and try on all the gear. But where is Susie? She's trying on a firefighter's hat! Can you find her?

Do you see a room with beds in it? That's where the firefighters sleep. They work in shifts that last all day and all night.

Can you find the kitchen? Firefighters work hard and get hungry! Then they go to the exercise room to keep in shape. Firefighters even have classrooms where they learn new things.

Look at the long, long hoses. The firefighters pump water through the hoses to put out fires. Then they hang them up to dry. Now find the room with the computer. That's where the call comes in when there's a fire. The firefighters come from all directions—even down the pole!—to jump on the trucks and scoot away. Clang! Clang! The firefighters are on their way!

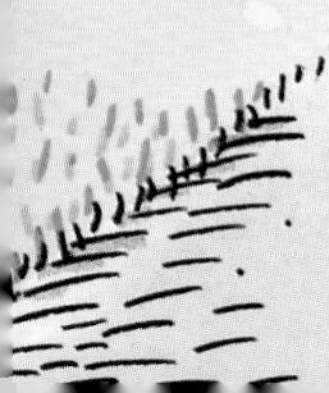

302
35

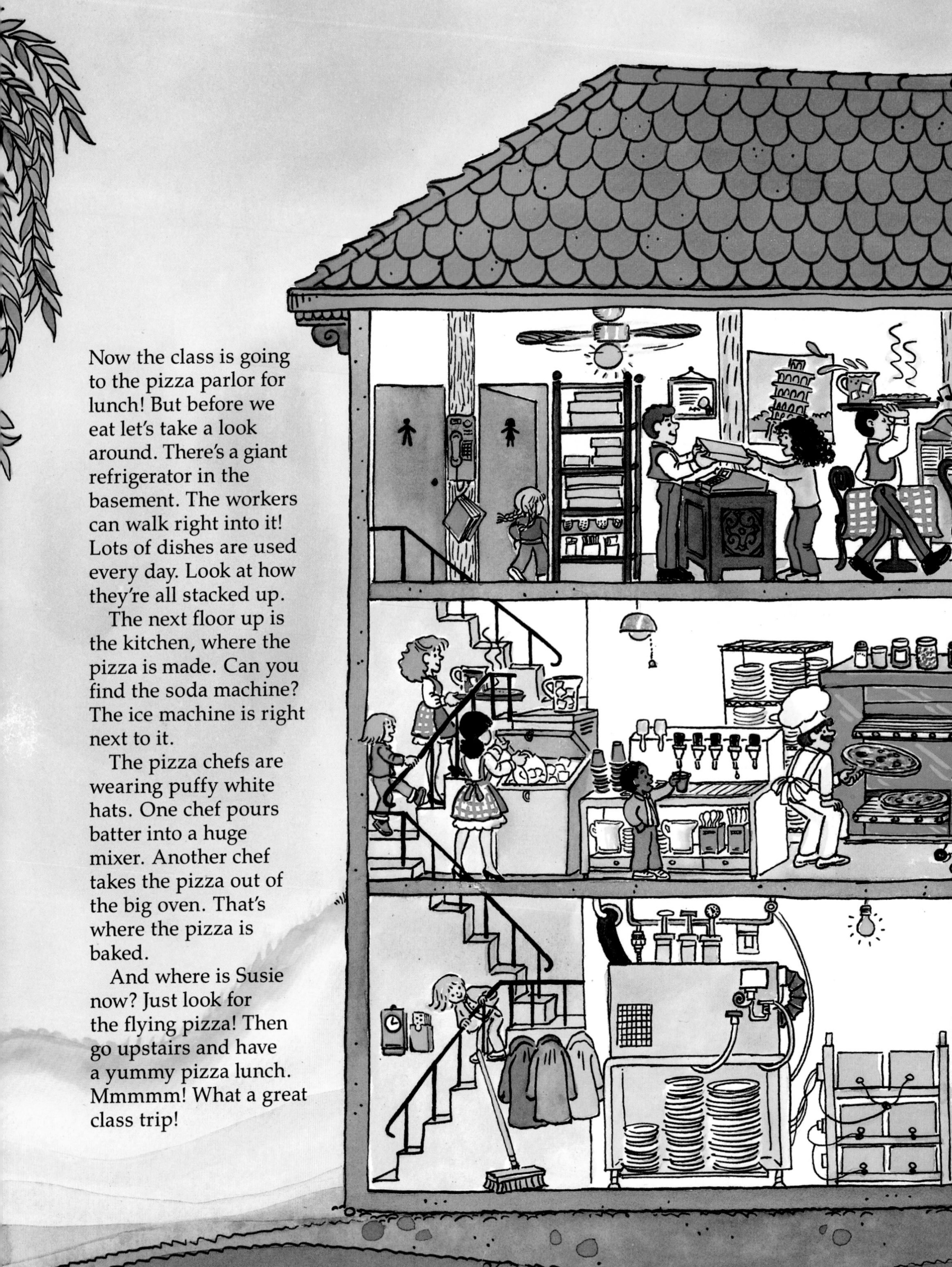

Now the class is going to the pizza parlor for lunch! But before we eat let's take a look around. There's a giant refrigerator in the basement. The workers can walk right into it! Lots of dishes are used every day. Look at how they're all stacked up.

The next floor up is the kitchen, where the pizza is made. Can you find the soda machine? The ice machine is right next to it.

The pizza chefs are wearing puffy white hats. One chef pours batter into a huge mixer. Another chef takes the pizza out of the big oven. That's where the pizza is baked.

And where is Susie now? Just look for the flying pizza! Then go upstairs and have a yummy pizza lunch. Mmmmm! What a great class trip!

Funny Jack

A Retelling of an English Folk Tale

This is the story of a funny boy named Jack. Jack lived with his mother on the edge of town. Jack's mother worked very hard, but she was very poor. All day long she worked her fingers to the bone, while Jack did nothing but lounge around the house.

One day Jack's mother said, "Jack, you're a big boy now. You're old enough to go out and get a job."

"A job?" said Jack. "But I don't know how to do anything!"

"You'll learn," said Jack's mother. "I need your help to pay the rent. I just can't afford to feed you anymore."

"Okay," said Jack. "First thing in the morning I'll go out and find some work."

So the next morning Jack got up early and walked into town. He stopped in all the shops and asked for work. Before long he found a job at the grocery store. "My bagger is out sick," said the man who owned the grocery store. "I will pay you one dollar to bag groceries today."

"It's a deal," said Jack, and he spent the day bagging groceries. When it was time to go home, the store owner paid him a dollar.

This was the very first dollar Jack had ever earned. He held it in his fingers and looked at it over and over as he walked home. But a few minutes later a gust of wind blew Jack's dollar right out of his hand and far away.

"Wow," said Jack. "Too bad."

When Jack got home his mother asked him if he had earned some money that day.

"I sure did," said Jack.

"Well, where is it?" asked his mother.

"The wind blew it right out of my hand," answered Jack.

"That's not funny, Jack," said his mother. "You should have put it in your pocket."

"Next time I will," said Jack.

The next day Jack walked into town again. This time he found work at a cheese shop. At the end of the day, the owner gave him some crumbly cheese to take home. Remembering what his mother had said, Jack immediately put the cheese in his pocket.

When he got home, he told his mother that he had earned some cheese that day.

"Good," said his mother. "We'll have it for dinner.'

Jack reached into his pocket to get the cheese. But it was all crumbled up and covered with lint from his pocket.

"That's not funny, Jack," said his mother. "You should have put it in a paper bag and carried it home in your hands."

"Next time, Mom," said Jack.

That night they had macaroni and cheese for dinner—without the cheese.

The next day Jack found a job at the pet store. At the end of the day the owner gave him a big tomcat. Remembering what his mother had said, Jack put the cat in a paper bag and carried it in his hands. But the cat didn't want to be put in a bag. It scratched its way out and ran away.

"Oh, well," said Jack. "You can't win them all."

When he got home, Jack told his mother about the cat.

"That's not funny, Jack!" cried his mother. "You should have put the cat on a leash and pulled it behind you."

"Next time, Mom," said Jack. "What's for supper?"

"Nothing," said his mother.

The next day Jack worked at a butcher shop. The owner paid him with a big, fat, juicy steak. "This is going to taste great tonight," Jack thought hungrily. Remembering what his mother had told him, he tied a string around the steak and pulled it behind him.

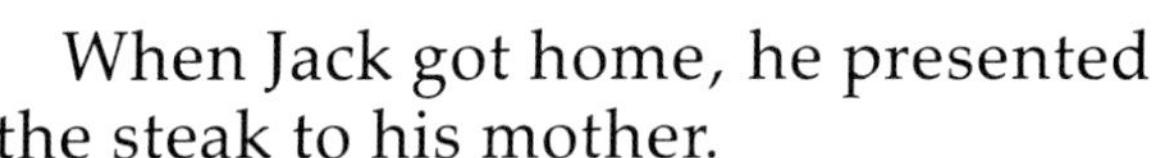

When Jack got home, he presented the steak to his mother.

"Ta da!"

But the steak was so dirty from being dragged on the ground that it was completely ruined.

"That's not funny, Jack!" said his mother. "You should have carried it on your shoulder!"

"Next time," said Jack.

The next day Jack worked at the horse stables. For his trouble, the owner gave him an old horse.

Remembering what his mother had told him, Jack lifted the horse up onto his shoulder. It wasn't easy, but somehow he managed to do it. The horse whinnied and kicked all the way.

"Hey," Jack said to the horse. "Hold still, will you?"

On his way home, Jack passed a manor house on a pond. It was owned by a rich man who had a pretty daughter. But the poor girl was very sick. She couldn't talk to save her life! Her father had called the best doctors around, but none of them could cure her. "She will never speak until someone makes her laugh," said the doctors. But the girl never ever laughed.

The girl happened to be sitting in the sun when Jack walked by. "Hi-de-ho!" called Jack as well as he could, considering he had a horse on his back with its legs kicking in the air. It was the funniest thing the girl had ever seen! All of a sudden she burst out laughing. And then she called out, "Hi-de-ho!"

The girl's father, hearing her voice, ran out to see what was happening. And when he saw his daughter laughing and talking with Jack, he jumped for joy.

Jack and the girl got married, and he and his mother moved into the manor house on the pond, where they played happily all day long. And whenever Jack did something silly—which was quite often—you can be sure that his wife just laughed and said, "You're so funny, Jack."

HEE-HEE-HEE-HEE
HEE-HEE-HEE-HEE

DENTIST

If I were a dentist,
(point to self)

I know what I would do.
(nod head)

I'd tell all the children,
"Brush your teeth,
(pretend to brush)

to keep your smile like new."
(smile)

And if a tiny hole should show,
(make a circle with fingers)

I'd say, "Climb in my chair."
I'd make my little drill go
"Buzzzzzzzzz."
I'd put a filling there.
(point to teeth)

BARBER

I hop into the barber's chair
(sit on a chair)

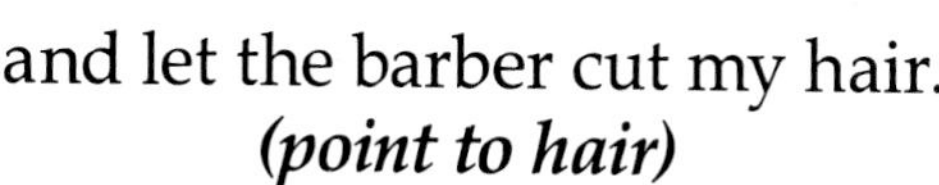

and let the barber cut my hair.
(point to hair)

"Zzzzzzzz," the barber's clippers go,
(pretend to cut hair)

sometimes fast and sometimes slow.
(move hands fast, then slowly)

I like it at our barber shop
because I get a lollipop!
(pretend to lick lollipop)

LET'S GO FOR A WALK

Walk through the neighborhood, look all around.
All kinds of wonderful things can be found!
A flower, a bird cage, a hat and a book —
There are interesting objects wherever you look!

Can you find these objects as you wander through the neighborhood?

- loaf of bread
- red book
- bird cage
- jump rope
- purple flower
- lemon
- paintbrush
- box of popcorn
- hat
- guitar
- dog

MOVIE
HOTEL
SCHOOL
LIBRARY

Living and Working Together

Neighborly

My Mother sends our neighbors things
On fancy little plates.
One day she sent them custard pie
And they sent back stuffed dates.

And once she sent them angel food
And they returned ice cream;
Another time for purple plums
They gave us devil's dream.

She always keeps enough for us
No matter what she sends.
Our goodies seem much better
When we share them with our friends.

And even if they didn't, why,
It's surely lots of fun,
'Cause that way we get two desserts
Instead of only one!

Violet Alleyn Storey

The Busy Bus

This is the bus that
  goes to town.

On comes the driver who
  drives the bus that
goes to town.

On comes a carpenter
  holding a hammer who
sits near the driver
  who drives the bus
that goes to town.

On comes a dancer who
  leaps and twirls,
passing the carpenter
  holding a hammer who
sits near the driver
  who drives the bus
that goes to town.

On comes a man who
  works at the deli and
brings a ham that
  falls on the floor, and
trips the dancer who
  leaps and twirls,
passing the carpenter
  holding a hammer who
sits near the driver
  who drives the bus
that goes to town.

On comes a nurse with a
polka-dot purse who
falls asleep on the
arm of the man who
works at the deli and
brings a ham that
falls on the floor, and
trips the dancer who
leaps and twirls,
passing the carpenter
holding a hammer who
sits near the driver
who drives the bus
that goes to town.

On comes a man with a
bird on his shoulder that
makes a loud squawk to
wake the nurse with a
polka-dot purse who
falls asleep on the
arm of the man who
works at the deli and
brings a ham that
falls on the floor, and
trips the dancer who
leaps and twirls,
passing the carpenter
holding a hammer who
sits near the driver
who drives the bus
that goes to town.

On comes a waitress who
doesn't like pets with
wings or beaks or
four sharp claws—she
sneers at the man with the
bird on his shoulder that
makes a loud squawk to
wake the nurse with a
polka-dot purse who
falls asleep on the
arm of the man who
works at the deli and
brings a ham that
falls on the floor, and
trips the dancer who
leaps and twirls,
passing the carpenter
holding a hammer who
sits near the driver
who drives the bus
that goes to town.

On comes an artist
who carries a paintbrush and
spills green paint on the knee
of the waitress who
doesn't like pets with
wings or beaks or
four sharp claws—she
sneers at the man with the
bird on his shoulder that
makes a loud squawk to
wake the nurse with a
polka-dot purse who
falls asleep on the
arm of the man who
works at the deli and
brings a ham that
falls on the floor, and
trips the dancer who
leaps and twirls,
passing the carpenter
holding a hammer who
sits near the driver
who drives the bus
that goes to town.

On comes a teacher with
fifteen young students who'll
spend their day at the
new art museum that's
showing the paintings
of the artist
who carries a paintbrush and
spills green paint on the knee
of the waitress who
doesn't like pets with
wings or beaks or
four sharp claws—she
sneers at the man with the
bird on his shoulder that
makes a loud squawk to
wake the nurse with a
polka-dot purse who
falls asleep on the
arm of the man who
works at the deli and
brings a ham that
falls on the floor, and
trips the dancer who
leaps and twirls,
passing the carpenter
holding a hammer who
sits near the driver
who drives the bus
that goes to town.

On comes a clown
from the circus in town
who tries to squeeze
three chimpanzees right
through the door, but
before they board, the
bus driver shouts,
"NO MORE ROOM!"

Wendy Wax

Neighbors

by H. L. Ross

Maple Leaf Lane was a friendly sort of neighborhood with kids living in almost every house. But the best thing about the neighborhood was the playground down at the end of the lane. It had the most wonderful wooden climber, with ropes to swing on and four tall towers to climb and three steep slides to go down and all sorts of nifty nooks and crannies.

Timothy and Hannah and Katy Rose lived on Maple Leaf Lane. They were neighbors and best friends. All three rode the same kind of scooter. All three loved peanut butter and ketchup sandwiches. And all three liked to play Space Explorers. The climber was their ship and their scooters were shuttlecraft. On Friday nights, when the ice-cream truck drove down Maple Leaf Lane with a cheery ding-ding-ding, they always got the same flavor—Double Chocolate Chip Dip Swirl. Everything was just terrific. . . until the day Hannah had to move away to another neighborhood.

As the moving truck pulled away, Timothy said, "I'm sure going to miss Hannah."

For a week after Hannah moved, they didn't play any of their favorite games. Nothing was as fun with two as it was with three. Then, one day, they saw a moving van pull into the driveway of Hannah's house, followed by a station wagon. A little girl, about their age, got out of the back of the station wagon. Timothy and Katy Rose got on their scooters and rode next door to meet her.

"Hi," said Timothy. "I'm Timothy and this is Katy Rose."

"Hi," said the girl. "I'm Erica and this is my new bike."

It was a brand-new, shiny red two-wheeler. "Wow!" said Katy Rose. She didn't ride her own two-wheeler very much because Hannah hadn't owned one and Timothy couldn't ride his yet.

"We like scooters better," Timothy said, and turned away.

"Want to come with us to the playground tomorrow?" Katy Rose asked.

"Sure!" said the new girl. "I saw it when we drove in."

The next morning, Katy Rose, Timothy, and Erica rode down the street to the playground. Erica took one look at the climber and said, "It looks like a castle!"

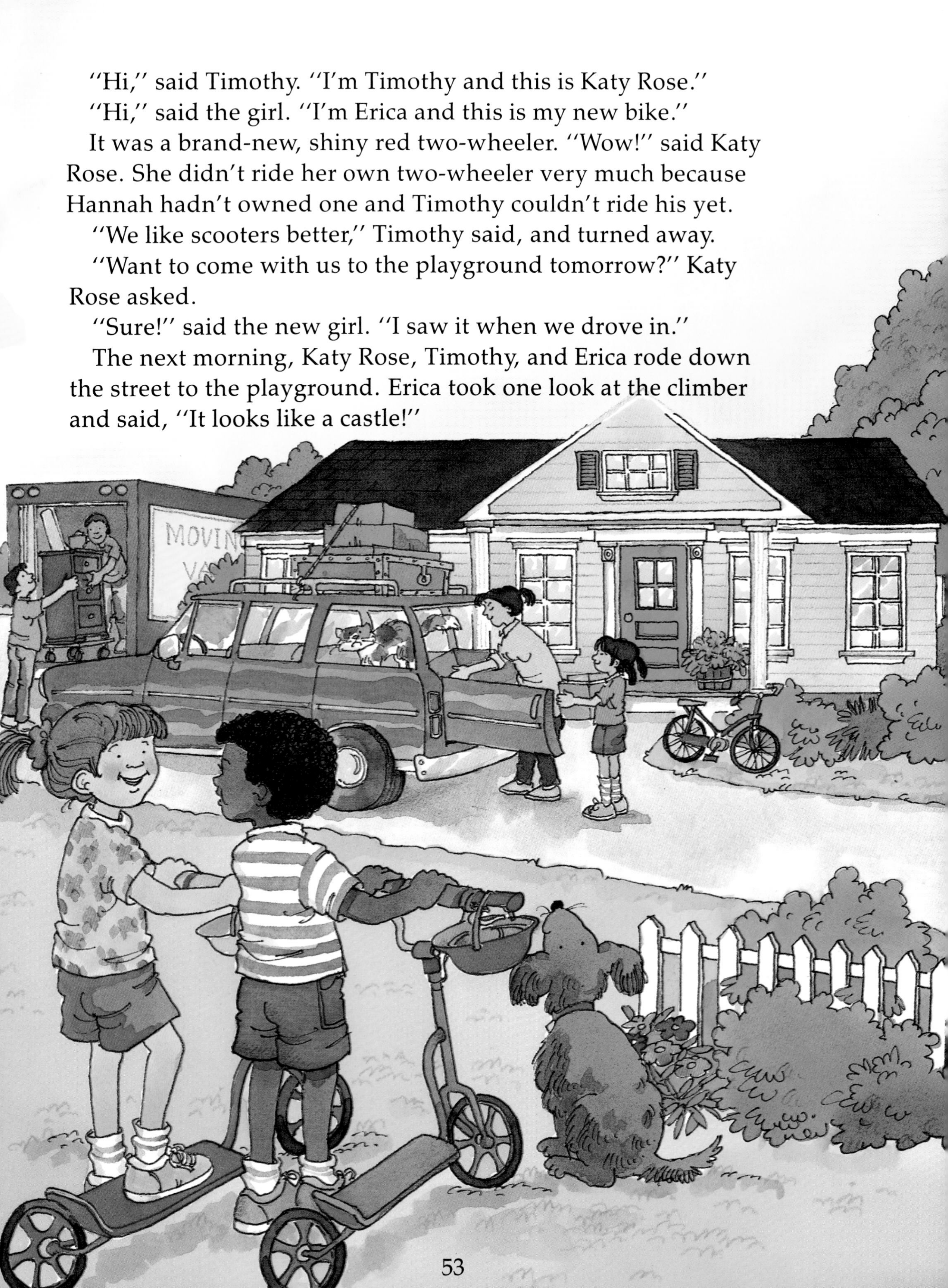

Katy Rose squinted at it. "It does . . . a little."

"No, it doesn't," Timothy said. "It looks like a spaceship. You want to play Space Explorers? The climber's the ship and our scooters are shuttlecraft. I guess you'll have to stay on the ship because you don't have a scooter."

"I'd rather play Castle!" said Erica. "My bike—and your scooters—can be horses!"

"I'm going home," said Timothy. "Are you coming, Katy Rose? We can have peanut butter and ketchup sandwiches."

"If you come to my house," said Erica, "you can have bologna."

Katy Rose didn't want to hurt anybody's feelings. So she said, "No thanks. I think I'll go home."

For a few days everybody just played by themselves. Nobody had much fun. So, Katy Rose went to the playground. Erica was up in one of the climber's towers, looking every bit as bored as Katy Rose. "Want to play Castle?" Katy Rose called up to her.

"You bet," Erica called down. "I'll even let you be Queen."

They played Castle all morning. Katy Rose had lunch at Erica's house. They had bologna sandwiches.

That afternoon, they met Timothy out on the sidewalk. He was wobbling all over the place trying to ride his two-wheeler.

"What you need," said Erica, "is a running push. That's how I learned. If you want, I'll give you one."

Timothy said yes and by dinnertime, with Erica's help, he was riding his two-wheeler.

The next day, all three of them rode to the playground on their bikes. They played Space Explorers in the morning and Castle in the afternoon.

"Erica's nice, isn't she?" Katy Rose said to Timothy on the way home, after they had dropped off their new friend at her house.

"She's okay," said Timothy. "But she's not Hannah."

"No. But it's kind of fun playing new games."

Timothy didn't say anything. But he thought about how Erica had helped him learn to ride his bike. After dinner, he heard the ding-ding-ding of the ice-cream truck. It gave him an idea. He ran to his piggy bank and got some money. Then he ran out to the truck and bought two Double Chocolate Chip Dip Swirls.

He went to Erica's house and knocked on the door. "You probably won't even like this," Timothy began when Erica answered his knock. But before he could finish, she said, "Mmmmm. Double Chocolate Chip Dip Swirl—my favorite flavor!"

Timothy's mouth dropped open. "Really?" Maybe Erica wasn't so different from Hannah, after all. Just then, Katy Rose walked up. She was licking a Double Chocolate Chip Dip Swirl. Timothy handed Erica one of the ice creams. "I just wanted to say . . . welcome to the neighborhood."

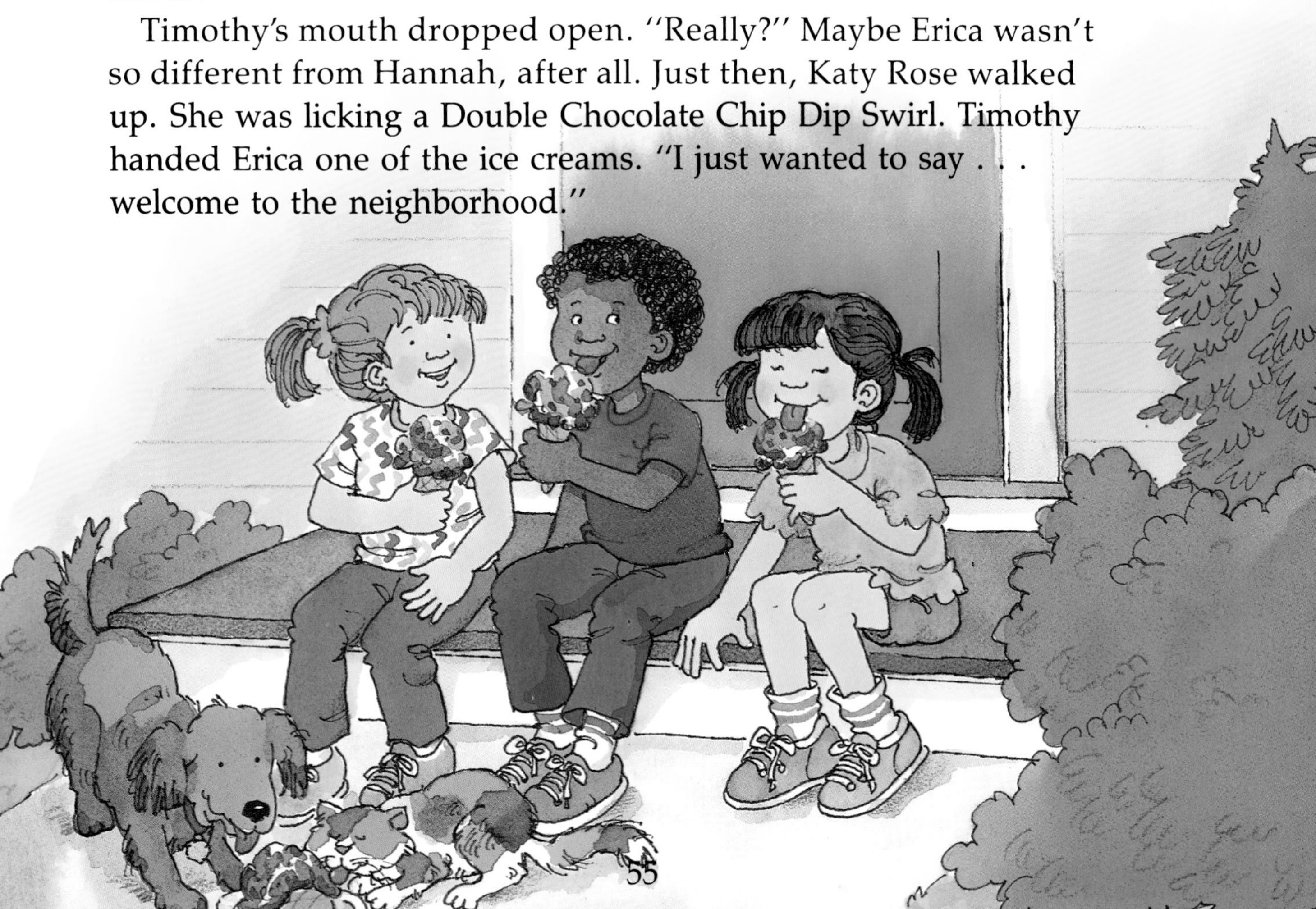

Doing a Good Deed

At the foot of the hill, the ice cream truck
Drove into a mudhole and got stuck.
We helped the driver back on the road.
But first we had to lighten the load.
When we had helped a gallon apiece,
The driver phoned the Chief of Police,
Who drove a pole into the sludge
And measured five feet of chocolate fudge
That had to be lightened. Well, we turned to
And helped the man. What else could we do?
I even called my Boy Scout Troop.
By then there was nothing left but soup.
Still, ice cream soup is very good.
And we wanted to help as much as we could.
It was our good deed for the day.
To help the man get on his way.
At last we pulled him out of the muck,
And he drove away in his empty truck,
Thanking us all for helping him out.
That made us happy. For there's no doubt
We must help our neighbor as much as we can.
Especially when he's the ice cream man.

John Ciardi

Stone Soup

A Retelling of a Traditional Folk Tale

Long ago, a hungry wanderer arrived in a village at supper time. "Ah, surely some kind person will give me something to eat," he said to himself.

The wanderer went to an old woman's hut and rapped on her door.

"What do you want?" she said.

"Excuse me, but I wonder if you could spare me some supper?" said the wanderer.

"I'm sorry," said the old woman, "but I have no food to give away." And with that, she closed her door.

More hungry than ever, the wanderer left the old woman's hut and went next door to a butcher shop.

"Excuse me," he said, "but I wonder if you could spare me some supper?"

"I'm sorry," said the butcher, "but we can't afford to give anything away in this neighborhood."

More hungry than ever, the wanderer left the butcher's and went across the road to a vegetable stall.

"Excuse me," he said to a farmer, "but I wonder if you could spare me some supper?"

"Sorry," said the farmer, "but we've all suffered a poor crop this year, and we can't give anything away."

"I see," said the wanderer.

So the wanderer sat under a tree and tried to think of what to do. He thought and thought until a smile slowly crossed his face. "Ah, of course," he said. "Stone soup."

The wanderer went back to the old woman's hut and rapped again on her door.

"What do you want now?" she said, peeking out.

"Excuse me," he said. "But I wonder if you could spare me a large cauldron?"

"What for?"

"I'd like to make some stone soup," he said.

"Stone soup?"

"Yes, and you're certainly invited to have some with me."

The old woman gave the wanderer an iron cauldron. She watched him drop a large stone into the pot. Then he filled the cauldron with water and put it over a fire. Soon the stone soup was bubbling over, and the wanderer sampled a spoonful.

"How's your soup?" said the old woman.

"Quite good," said the wanderer, "though it might be a bit tastier with some potatoes."

"Potatoes? I have potatoes," said the old woman. "Wait a minute."

A moment later the old woman tossed a dozen potatoes into the soup cauldron.

"What are you making?" called the farmer from across the road.

"Stone soup," said the wanderer.

"Stone soup? What's in it?"

"A stone and some potatoes," said the wanderer. "It's quite good, though it might be a bit tastier with some carrots and onions."

"Carrots and onions?" said the farmer. "I have carrots and onions. Wait a minute."

A moment later, the farmer brought a bunch of carrots and onions to the soup cauldron and threw them in.

The farmer's wife then called from across the road. "What are you making?"

"Stone soup," said the wanderer.

"What's in it?" asked the farmer's wife.

"A stone, some potatoes, carrots, and onions," said the wanderer. "It's quite good, though it might be a bit tastier with some pepper and barley."

"Oh, I have some pepper and barley," said the farmer's wife.

"Wait a minute."

A moment later, the farmer's wife brought some pepper and barley to the soup cauldron and threw them in.

Soon the butcher called from his shop. "What smells so good?"

"Stone soup," said the wanderer.

"What's in it?"

"A stone, some potatoes, carrots, onions, pepper, and barley. It's quite good," said the wanderer, "though it might be a bit tastier with a chicken."

"I have a chicken," said the butcher. "Wait a minute."

A moment later, the butcher threw a fresh chicken into the soup cauldron.

"All we need now are some bowls," said the wanderer.

"Bowls coming up," said the farmer's wife.

"And spoons?" said the wanderer.

"Indeed, here are spoons," said the farmer.

"And something to drink?" said the wanderer.

"Cold cider! Plenty of it!" said the old woman.

"Crusty bread and butter?" said the wanderer.

"Here, here," said the butcher.

In the evening twilight, the farmer, the farmer's wife, the old woman, the butcher, and the wanderer all had a feast. They ate the delicious stone soup and the good crusty bread and drank plenty of cold cider.

After dinner the butcher played his mandolin. The old woman sang a song about friends, and the farmer's wife and the farmer danced their feet off.

They all laughed, talked, danced, and sang through the night.

"This is the first time I've ever spent time with you good neighbors," said the old woman to the butcher, the farmer, and his wife.

"We'll have to do this again!" said the farmer.

As dawn was breaking, all the neighbors shook hands and vowed to meet at least once a month to have stone soup.

"Thank you for everything!" they said to the wanderer.

"Thank you," he said. Then he picked up his stone and waved good-bye. And feeling full and happy, he walked toward the sun rising over the hills.

Little People™ Big Book About WHERE WE LIVE

TIME-LIFE for CHILDREN™

Publisher: Robert H. Smith
Managing Editor: Neil Kagan
Associate Editors: Jean Burke Crawford, Patricia Daniels
Marketing Director: Ruth P. Stevens
Promotion Director: Kathleen B. Tresnak
Associate Promotion Director: Jane B. Welihozkiy
Production Manager: Prudence G. Harris
Editorial Consultants: Jacqueline A. Ball, Sara Mark

PRODUCED BY PARACHUTE PRESS, INC.

Editorial Director: Joan Waricha
Editors: Christopher Medina, Jane Stine, Wendy Wax
Writers: Ted Bailey, Cathy Dubowski, Gail Herman, H.L. Ross, Thelma Slater, Natalie Standiford, Jean Waricha, Wendy Wax
Designer: Deborah Michel
Illustrators: Yvette Banek: 16-21, 30-31, 56-57; Shirley Beckes: 22-25, 44-45; Stephanie Britt: 8-13; Ann Iosa: 52-55; Hilary Knight: 14-15; Diane Palmisciano: 28-29; Roz Schanzer: 32-37; John Speirs: cover, 4-5, 26-27, 38-41, 46-47; John Wallner: 48-51, 58-63; Linda Weller: 6-7, 42-43.

First printing. Printed in U.S.A.
Published simultaneously in Canada.

Time-Life Books Inc. is a wholly owned subsidiary of THE TIME INC. BOOK COMPANY.

ACKNOWLEDGMENTS

Every effort has been made to trace the ownership of all copyrighted material and to secure the necessary permissions to reprint these selections. If any question arises as to the use of any material, the editor and the publisher, while expressing regret for any inadvertent error, will make the necessary correction in future printings.

Grateful acknowledgment is made to the following for permission to reprint the copyrighted material listed below: Greenwillow Books (a division of William Morrow Co.) for "Lavinia Nink" from THE NEW KID ON THE BLOCK by Jack Prelutsky. Copyright © 1984 by Jack Prelutsky. Homeland Publishing, a division of Troubador Records for "The Corner Grocery Store" from THE RAFFI SINGABLE SONG BOOK; traditional, adopted lyrics by Raffi and D. Pike. Copyright © 1979 by Homeland Publishing. Houghton Mifflin Co. for "Doing A Good Deed" from DOODLE SOUP by John Ciardi. Copyright © 1985 by Myra J. Ciardi. Original illustrations copyright © 1985 by Merle Nacht. Barbara Huff for "The Library." Judson Press for "Barber" and "Dentist" from FINGERPLAY FRIENDS by Audrey Olson Leighton. Copyright © 1984 by Judson Press. Morrow Jr. (a division of William Morrow Co.) for "In My Neighborhood" from SUBWAY SWINGER by Virginia Schonborg. Copyright © 1970 by Virginia Schonborg. Rand McNally & Co. for "Neighborly" by Violet Alleyn Storey. Copyright © 1926, 1954 by Rand McNally & Co. Scholastic, Inc. for THE BIG ORANGE SPLOT by D. Manus Pinkwater. Copyright © 1977 by D. Manus Pinkwater. Dorothy Brown Thompson for "Our House."

Library of Congress Cataloging-in-Publication Data

Little people big book about where we live.
p. cm. —(Little people big books)
Summary: A collection of original stories, traditional tales, essays, poems, songs, activities, and games, grouped under the headings "My House and Your House," "Around the Corner & Down the Street," and "Living and Working Together."
ISBN 0-8094-7483-2. — ISBN 0-8094-7484-0 (lib. bdg.)
1. City and town life—Literary collections. 2. Neighborliness—Literary collections. [1. City and town life—Literary collections. 2. Neighborliness—Literary collections.] I. Time-Life for Children (Firm) II. Series.
PZ5.L72594 1990 808.8'0355—dc20 89-49494 CIP AC

TIME-LIFE BOOKS
ALEXANDRIA, VIRGINIA

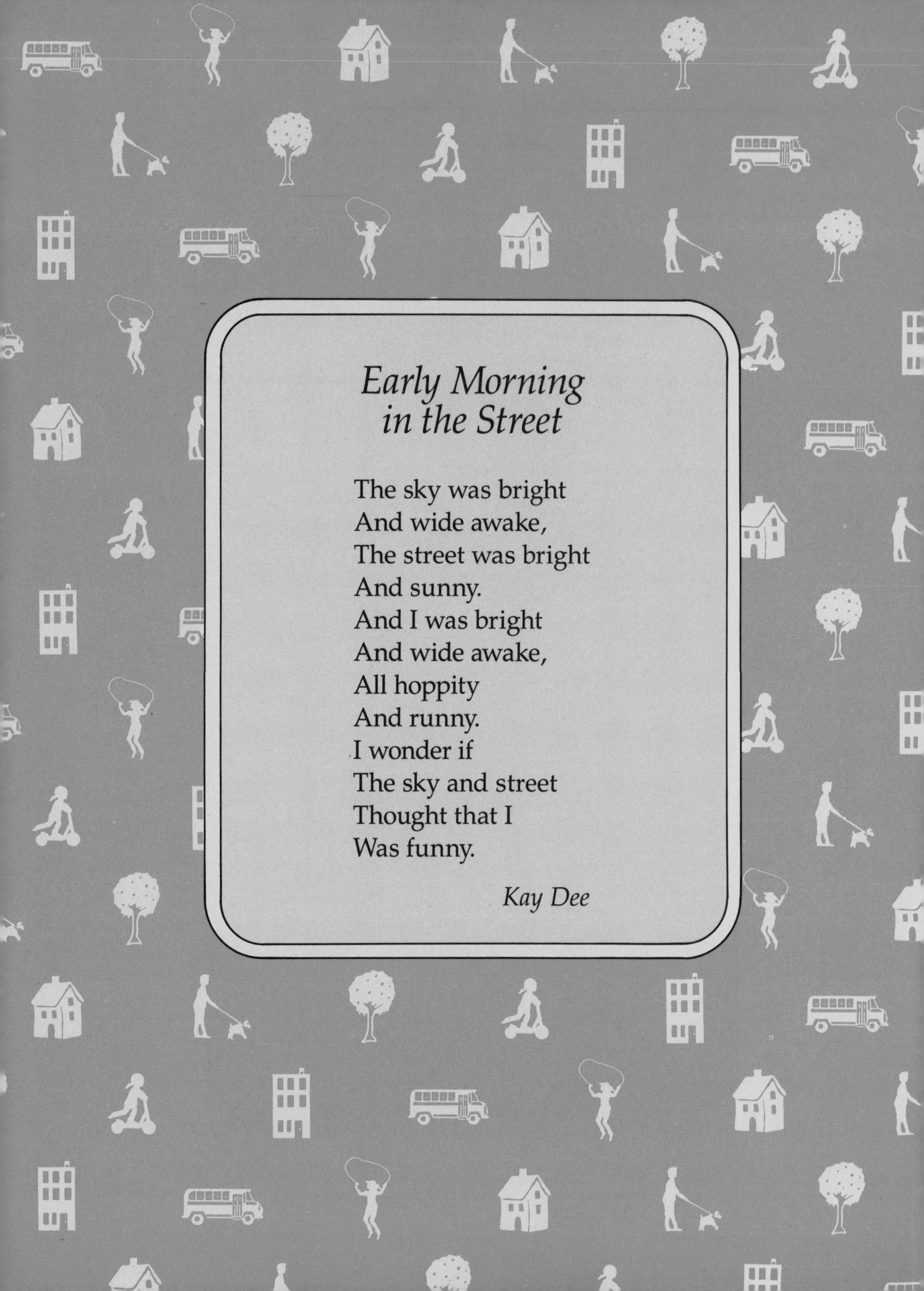

Early Morning in the Street

The sky was bright
And wide awake,
The street was bright
And sunny.
And I was bright
And wide awake,
All hoppity
And runny.
I wonder if
The sky and street
Thought that I
Was funny.

Kay Dee